EXECUTIVE SEARCH
AND
YOUR CAREER

*The BlueSteps® Guide to
Career Management*

Association of Executive Search Consultants

NEW YORK

EXECUTIVE SEARCH AND YOUR CAREER
The BlueSteps® Guide to Career Management

This volume is part of the AESC Executive Search Series.

Acknowledgements

Writing and publishing this book has been accomplished through a team effort.

The AESC's thanks go to Tom Gorman of Content Publishing Services for his assistance in drafting and editing the manuscript.

Thanks to Della Giles, Kunal Dutta and Jo Elliot of the AESC staff who were instrumental in the beginning stages of the project and who produced the outline and content research for the book.

AESC would like to thank the members of the AESC Board of Directors for their input, and Matt Helbing for book and cover design. Thanks also to Kathryn Braine for managing the final stages of editing and production, and to Ellen Adamson for professional guidance with copy editing.

Finally, thanks to Christine Hayward, who provided the overall management and drive to get the project completed—as we all know, execution is everything.

Peter Felix
AESC President

ABOUT THE ASSOCIATION OF EXECUTIVE SEARCH CONSULTANTS

The Association of Executive Search Consultants is the worldwide professional association for retained executive search consulting firms. The AESC's mission is to promote the highest professional standards in retained executive search consulting, broaden public understanding of the executive search process, and serve as an advocate for the interests of its member firms. For more information, or to download the AESC Code of Ethics and Professional Practice Guidelines, go to www.aesc.org.

ABOUT BLUESTEPS®

BlueSteps® is an online career management service providing executives continual exposure to the world's top search firms. As an exclusive service of the AESC, BlueSteps enables executives to efficiently and confidentially remain accessible to all member firms of the AESC. For more information, go to www.bluesteps.com.

Contents

Introduction

A huge range of profit and nonprofit enterprises have come to rely on retained executive search firms to fill their most senior positions. Although they once worked mainly with major corporations and financial institutions, search firms now also recruit talent in fields as diverse as education, health care, arts management and government. Moreover, the executive search profession, like many of the organizations it serves, has become global.

Yet even sophisticated executives often misunderstand basic aspects of retained executive search. Many managers fail to see the role that search consultants could play potentially in their careers, while others misinterpret that role. Unfortunately, few executives know how to increase their visibility among executive search professionals—visibility that could bring them to positions they would never even be aware of if not for a search consultant's phone call.

This book addresses those knowledge gaps. It explains retained executive search as a business and a process, and shows potential candidates how to work well with search professionals. Of course, for a manager to become a candidate in a search, certain elements must be in place. Chief among these is a record of outstanding performance in increasingly challenging positions. A bit of luck doesn't hurt. But knowledge always helps, which is why we've written this book.

Here you will learn how to capitalize on the fact that thousands of organizations retain executive search firms to recruit men and women for senior positions every year. When you know how executive search consultants work, you can maximize your chances of becoming a candidate for a position being filled by a search firm—and of working effectively with a consultant. Also, if you happen to be in a hiring organization, this book will deepen your knowledge of the rigorous recruitment process that search professionals conduct for clients like yourself.

This book is presented by the Association of Executive Search Consultants (AESC), the worldwide professional association for retained executive search firms. AESC members are well-established retained executive search firms who have committed themselves to the highest standards of professional practice. You can learn more about the AESC and its member firms at www.aesc.org.

Successful careers don't just happen. They are built and managed, step-by-step. If you received this book through your membership in BlueSteps®, you have already taken one step toward becoming more visible to the search community. BlueSteps® is the AESC's online career-management service, which makes information on senior executives available online to retained executive search consultants at AESC member firms. BlueSteps® gives prospective candidates one way of staying on the radar screens of retained executive search firms. This book will provide you with many more.

CHAPTER 1

Executive Search and Your Career

The retained executive search profession has grown exponentially over the past two decades, yet it remains mysterious to many managers and other professionals. For instance, many people confuse executive search firms with employment agencies. Others believe that executive search consultants recruit only corporate CEOs or high-profile executives regularly covered in the business press. Some managers even believe that executive search consultants "find jobs" for executives, when as this book will show, that is not the case.

This book will clear up these and many other points. More importantly, it will show you how to attract the attention of executive search professionals and how to interact effectively with them at every stage of a search. Those are worthwhile career-management skills, especially now. Managerial job mobility has never been greater, and shows no signs of abating. If anything, executive turnover—both voluntary and involuntary—continues to mount under the pressures of global competition, economic uncertainty and demand for performance.

Most executives understand that they must actively manage their careers. However, many don't see the role that executive search can play in that endeavor. While it may not be as large as that of other career management tactics such as acquiring a well-rounded skill set and timing your career moves properly, don't underestimate the role that a search firm could play in your career. Many men and women at the top of their professions reached those heights with a boost from an executive search consultant.

Let's start with a look at what executive search firms do.

WHAT IS (AND ISN'T) EXECUTIVE SEARCH?

An executive search firm works with its client—the hiring organization—to fill a position with the *best person* for that position. This differs sharply from the goal of filling the position with the best *available* person. An executive search firm commits itself to locating and recruiting the best person, regardless of whether he or she is already employed or seeking a new position.

This approach broadens and deepens the talent pool available to a search firm's clients. A search firm doesn't run a help-wanted ad and recruit candidates from the self-selected group of people who see the ad and then answer it. Nor does the search firm limit itself to combing through its file of resumes. Instead, executive search consultants actively seek and recruit the most highly qualified candidates for a given position. Consultants will even recruit a specific individual that the client would like to consider, regardless of whether that person is seeking a position.

As a potential candidate you must grasp the distinction between retained executive search firms and other recruiting or placement services. There are four key distinctions:

- Retained executive search firms work with client organizations to fill *senior level* management or specialized professional positions. An executive search is not an economically feasible strategy for filling lower level positions.

- Retained executive search firms work with clients on an *exclusive basis*. This means that only one search firm—and no other firm or agency—is working to fill that position.

- Retained executive search firms are *retained by the client organization* to fill the position. This means that the client pays the search firm to mount the search and present the most qualified candidates. Some portion of the search firm's fee is typically paid before the search begins—hence, the term "retained executive search." (More on that later in this chapter.)

- As the title indicates, a retained executive search consultant plays a *consultative role*, working with clients to define positions, qualifications and potential sources of talent. The consultant will also offer insights regarding the compensation package required to attract certain types of candidates.

Just as executive search firms have their role to play, so do employment agencies, career counselors and outplacement consultants. For instance, organizations that offer career and outplacement services help individuals develop their career goals and job search skills, often when they've been laid off or fired. By contrast, executive search consultants, known informally as "headhunters," resemble talent scouts. Like scouts for sports teams and Hollywood studios, executive search consultants seek and recruit the extremely talented people that their clients require.

ADVANTAGES OF EXECUTIVE SEARCH FIRMS

Executive search firms deliver value to both hiring organizations and potential candidates for positions. The advantages to the hiring organization are:

- *Confidentiality:* Positions filled by search firms are rarely advertised by either the hiring organization or the search firm. This is an advantage for hiring organizations who want to avoid telling the world, or even their industry, that they are recruiting. A search consultant will often withhold a client's identity, even from a potential candidate, until the candidate's qualifications and interest have been established.

- *Expertise:* Executive search consultants usually specialize in a specific industry, such as financial services, or a specific function, such as IT management. As a result, they develop deep expertise in their area. Their daily interactions and network of contacts give them a unique, close-up perspective on their specialty's senior-level job market. The search consultant can therefore help an organization define the position, qualifications and compensation package in realistic but attractive terms.

- *Professionalism:* Once a somewhat "clubby" business, executive search has grown into one of the most competitive professions. Established search consultants have proven themselves in an arena packed with demanding clients, where intelligence, judgment and integrity are intrinsic.

Potential candidates benefit from working with search consultants in the following ways:

- *Access to a "hidden" job market:* Because search consultants recruit for positions that are rarely advertised, they give candidates access to what might be termed a hidden job market of challenging, high-level, well-compensated positions. Incidentally, your pursuit of a new position also remains hidden; conversations with an executive recruiter occur in private.

- *Solid Information:* If you are recruited, the search consultant will describe the position and the hiring organization in depth before your interviews. You walk into an interview at a company fully prepared for an informative, two-way conversation.

- *Advantageous Positioning:* If a search consultant arranges an interview for you, you have cleared a formidable hurdle. A consultant usually speaks with dozens of potential candidates to find a half-dozen to present to the client. Of course, the other candidates in the search process have cleared the same hurdle. However, even if you don't receive an offer, having been recruited provides experience that you'll find valuable the next time you enter a job search.

All of that said, please understand that a search consultant *works for the hiring organization*: that is, for his client. Consultants do not "find positions" for candidates. Nor do they counsel candidates on their career goals or their next career step, except in context of the hiring organization's needs. While consultants offer candidates tips on interviewing at the hiring organization, they are not in the business of coaching people on job search or career management skills, although they have the ability to do so. Executive search consultants keep their clients' interests uppermost in their minds. So if a consultant ever seems guarded in providing information or advice, don't take it personally. They are simply maintaining their focus.

ABOUT RETAINED EXECUTIVE SEARCH

By its nature, executive search calls for diplomacy, social skills and sensitivity on the one hand, and on the other hand, tenacity, negotiating skills and objective business judgment. Although search consultants are often viewed as "sales types," the search profession is actually a form of consulting, hence the title "executive search consultant."

Some candidates and even some hiring executives believe that search firms "sell" candidates to the hiring company. Wrong! If anything, they sell the company to qualified candidates. But, in fact, search firms sell neither candidates nor companies—they sell executive search services. This is particularly true in retained executive search engagements. In essence, the retained search firm says to the client:

> *We know your industry and the function of the position you want to fill. We understand the job market and the qualifications for the position. We have the resources to help you define the scope of the search. We will launch a search for executives who meet the position's qualifications and will include any internal and external candidates that you identify. We will locate, evaluate and actively recruit qualified candidates who can mesh with your organizational culture.*
>
> *These are the services you are purchasing. If the search is incomplete for reasons beyond our control or if you do not hire one of the qualified candidates we recruit, we have still expended resources and provided a valuable service. The retainer you pay us pays for those resources and services.*

A small portion of senior executive searches does not result in a placement. Rarely, if ever, does this occur because the search firm failed to locate and present qualified candidates. Usually the reasons involve the hiring company's redefining or eliminating the position for budgetary or organizational reasons. As you may imagine, changes in internal politics, priorities or reporting lines can radically alter the scope of a position to be filled, even during a search. In such situations a retainer relationship ensures that the executive search firm is compensated for its work, even though the position was eliminated, altered or not filled by the hiring organization.

THE BUSINESS OF RETAINED SEARCH

Retained executive search consulting is recognized today as a key management tool which helps organizations around the world recruit talented and skilled executives for critical appointments.

The demand for executive search has grown rapidly over the past several decades until it is a worldwide profession with revenues approaching $8 billion per annum. There are few organizations, for profit or non-profit, that don't use executive search from time to time. These include hospitals, sports organizations, charities, government bodies, and religious institutions as well as companies both large and small.

Such is the nature of the executive market in the developed economies of the world that the demand for executive search consulting is only likely to increase further. Executive mobility, the competitive environment and changing demographics are all contributing to a demand for executive talent that is growing rather than diminishing.

At one time or another most senior executives will encounter executive search in their careers. This book will help you when you do.

CHAPTER 2

How Retained Executive Search Works

A hiring organization usually retains an executive search firm only for its most mission-critical senior positions. The annual *base salary* offered often exceeds $250,000 and almost never comes in below $100,000, or the equivalent in non-U.S. currency. The hiring authority will be a senior manager of the company or division, and one or more senior managers must usually approve the hire. For most senior positions, such as chief executive officer and chief operating officer, the board of directors or a search committee, or both, may be involved in the hiring decision.

In other words, there's a lot at stake in a retained executive search—for the hiring organization, the search firm and the candidate. The success of a search depends on a successful relationship among these parties, and the search consultant choreographs key aspects of this relationship. However, the client—the hiring organization—always makes the hiring decision.

In this chapter we look at how organizations use retained executive search, at the structure and work of a search firm, and at the search process itself.

INFORMATION + INTEGRITY = EXECUTIVE SEARCH

An executive search firm runs on information. That includes information about specific industries; companies and their strategies and cultures; and executives and their strengths, weaknesses, backgrounds and salaries. Search firms employ various sources of information, which we'll examine in Chapter 3. Among the most important of these are contacts in the industries, disciplines and companies in which the search firm operates. Thus, all search professionals spend a good deal of time networking among valuable sources of information.

A retained executive search firm also represents the hiring organization in the recruitment effort. While search consultants may keep their client's identity confidential for as long as possible, they eventually reveal it to potential candidates, which of course links the search firm to a given organization.

In this context, retained executive search consultants must operate with the highest levels of integrity and with sensitivity to the needs of all parties. For this reason, AESC member firms agree to uphold the Professional Practice Guidelines you will find at www.aesc.org. All member firms of the AESC subscribe to these standards of professional practice.

WHO DOES WHAT IN A SEARCH FIRM?

Although there are firms consisting of two or three individuals, mid-size to large executive search firms include professionals at three levels: 1) presidents, partners and practice leaders 2) search consultants and associates and 3) researchers.

- *Presidents and partners* manage the search firm, develop new business and manage client relationships. In a small firm, the president/owner may share some of these functions with search consultants. *Practice leaders* perform these functions for a practice within a larger firm such as financial services or IT.

- *Search consultants* manage searches and client relationships and develop new business. On an executive search, consultants work closely with clients to define the position and its requirements and to interview and evaluate potential candidates. *Associates* perform some of the functions of search consultants, but usually with less experience and seniority. In some firms they also conduct research and work with candidates. Associates are typically on a career path that can lead to the position of search consultant (and perhaps partner or practice leader). During a search, consultants and associates evaluate potential candidates located by researchers.

- *Researchers* tap a wide variety of sources to locate candidates for a position. When you are recruited by a search firm, the researcher is typically the first person who will contact you. In that conversation the researcher will attempt to verify your general suitability for, and interest in, the position. (We'll discuss how to handle that phone call in Chapter 4.) The researcher then passes the interested candidates' names on to an associate or search consultant for further evaluation. While some researchers become associates or, eventually, search consultants, many prefer to remain "behind the scenes" in this information-gathering role.

Search professionals come from a wide variety of educational and employment backgrounds. Many have managerial experience in the industries or disciplines for which they recruit. Others have worked in corporate human resources departments, for instance in recruiting or compensation analysis. There is no "typical" background for a search professional. Yet successful search consultants tend to have several characteristics in common. They are generally good communicators, are well organized, have excellent interpersonal and problem-solving skills and tend to be articulate, analytical, empathetic and energetic.

THE SEARCH BEGINS

When an organization decides to retain an executive search firm, it may or may not have a past or ongoing relationship with that firm. When a hiring organization does maintain a relationship with a search firm, the firm's consultants become quite familiar with the organization's structure, culture, management and expectations. This can enhance the firm's effectiveness on a search. However, regardless of the search firm's familiarity with the hiring company, a search always begins with a definition of the position and its requirements.

The search consultant will ascertain if the hiring organization has addressed the following questions and, if appropriate, will consult with management to resolve them:

- What is the function of the job and its place in the structure of the organization? What are the strategic and tactical challenges of the job?

- Is this a new or an existing position? If an existing position, is it currently filled or has it been vacated?

- What are the requirements for success in the position in terms of experience, education and personal qualities?

- Are there internal candidates for the position? Will these people be considered in addition to external candidates?

- Does the organization believe that significantly better candidates can be found in the market than from within? Is the organization committed to finding the best possible candidate?

- How soon must the position be filled? What is the envisioned time frame of the search?

- What is the compensation package? How is the compensation structured in terms of base salary, bonuses or other incentives (such as stock or stock options) and benefits? Is this compensation realistic?

• Does the company understand how the executive search process works?

When an organization retains an executive search firm, both parties usually sign a retainer agreement. This confirms the client's commitment to the assignment, the search firm's exclusive right to represent the client in recruiting for the position, and items such as reference checking and nondisclosure of confidential information. As noted in Chapter 1, a retainer agreement represents a consulting contract, and successful performance is not defined by the placement of an external candidate in the position.

As a candidate, you should ascertain whether a position you are being recruited for is being filled on a retained basis. This will affect the way your candidacy is handled, the quality of the information you receive and your access to the hiring organization's senior management.

THE BRIEFING DOCUMENT: DEFINING THE POSITION

Once the retainer agreement has been signed, the search firm will develop a briefing document that sets the parameters for the search. The briefing document is shaped by the search consultant's in-depth conversations with key people in the hiring organization. This document includes a detailed job specification, description of the organization, and the experience and personal qualities desired in the candidate.

The briefing document serves as the "North Star" for everyone involved. The researchers at the search firm refer to the document as they seek potential candidates.

Both the search consultant and the hiring authorities use it to frame interview questions. The consultant will often share the briefing document with qualified, interested candidates, who should refer to it in preparing for the interviews.

As a potential candidate, you should ask to see a copy of the briefing document. If you are told that you cannot see it or that none exists, politely ask why. In some cases, issues of confidentiality may preclude sharing or even creating a briefing document. However, if you don't see the briefing document, conduct a bit of research to satisfy yourself regarding the credentials and status of the search firm.

HOW DOES THE EXECUTIVE SEARCH PROCESS WORK?

In general, the *client organization* can expect the following services from a retained executive search firm, which also reflect the sequence of the search:

- Meeting with the client to develop an understanding of the organization's structure, culture and needs as well as the position's requirements.

- Signing the retainer agreement and creating the briefing document, which together identify the requirements of the position, scope of services, search manager, general timetable, fees, expenses and cancellation policy.

- Conducting thorough, independent research to locate qualified potential candidates for the position.

- Submitting verbal and written reports on the progress of the search, including feedback from the marketplace. (This is an important, but often overlooked, service of search firms.)

- Evaluating potential candidates by interviewing them, verifying their credentials and assessing their strengths and weaknesses.

- Preparing and submitting written reports and evaluations of short-listed candidates prior to their interviews with the client.

- Before a candidate is offered the position, conducting a comprehensive reference check on behalf of the client.

- Conveying the offer to the candidate, participating in the negotiations and facilitating communication to maximize the client's chances of recruiting the first-choice candidate.

- Following-up with both client and candidate after the starting date and, if necessary, helping to integrate the candidate into the new job and corporate environment.

Retained search firms tend to perform these services more efficiently and effectively than the hiring organization can, while acting as a buffer between the client and the candidates. In subsequent chapters, we will discuss ways of dealing with the search consultant and the hiring organization at these various stages of the search process.

There are several other factors to consider when working with a retained search firm, as a candidate or as a hiring authority:

- A retained search consultant will not present a candidate to more than one client simultaneously unless there are exceptional circumstances and all parties involved have agreed to this course of action.

- A search consultant will not accept fees from executives to provide career advice or help them find a job.

- While search consultants work for the client company, they also build professional relationships with candidates. Consultants often remain in touch with candidates for years, even decades, over the course of their careers.

- In a successful search, all parties—consultant, client and candidate—fully understand their rights, responsibilities and obligations to each other.

In a search, you become a candidate *only after* the consultant has conducted an initial evaluation of your qualifications and you have expressed an interest in the position.

WHAT YOU SHOULD EXPECT

As a candidate, you should expect the following when you deal with a retained executive search consultant. (This section is adapted from AESC's *Candidate's Bill of Rights*, see Appendix.)

- *Confidentiality:* When you become a candidate for a new position, you assume some risk that your current employer may learn about it. You are therefore entitled to the highest levels of confidentiality from the search firm and the hiring organization.

- *Full Disclosure:* To make the right decision, you must be given all the information you need regarding the search firm, hiring organization and position. (However, during your first conversation, you are a potential candidate, and the search consultant need not divulge sensitive information about the client or the position at this stage.)

- *Professional Treatment:* The search consultant should have a clear understanding of the position and its requirements as well as the organization's culture. The consultant should answer your questions honestly, be organized and prepared, and respect the time you are investing.

- *Adequate Process Details:* The search consultant should tell you about the time frame of the search, the steps that lie ahead and the people you will meet before a decision is made.

- *No Pressure:* The best executive placements occur when the candidate has time to make a thoughtful decision. A search consultant should never try to hurry your decision or pressure you to accept an offer. The consultant should, however, inform you of deadlines and the implications of making or not making a timely decision.

Candidates working with a retained executive search consultant clearly enjoy several benefits. While it's true that search consultants represent the interests of their clients—the hiring organizations—they also work to ensure the best fit between candidate and company. (That is in the client's *and* the candidate's best interests.) A consultant will therefore evaluate that fit along with a candidate's qualifications for the position. He will also supply valuable information during the interview process, including insights into the corporate culture and, usually, the people you will be meeting in your interviews.

Bear in mind that it is your responsibility to present yourself properly in all interviews and negotiations. Even so, working with a retained search consultant gives you the point of view of a professional who knows the client, job market and position better than you do, without being an employee of the hiring organization.

Now let's turn to ways of attracting the attention of executive search consultants (the subject of Chapter 3).

ACTION POINTS

- If a search consultant approaches you as a candidate for a position, ask whether the position is being filled on a retained basis. This affects the handling of your candidacy, the information you receive and your access to senior management.

- As a candidate, ask to see a copy of the briefing document, which defines the scope and duties of the position. In some cases, the search firm cannot share the briefing document—or none may exist—due to issues of confidentiality. But if there is a briefing document, you have solid information on the position and its place in the organization, so be sure to request it.

- As a candidate working with a retained executive search consultant, you should expect confidentiality, full disclosure, professional treatment, adequate details on the hiring process and no pressure to accept an offer.

- Remember that the search consultant represents the hiring organization and that it is your responsibility to represent your interests.

However, search consultants try to ensure the best fit between candidates and clients, and they see relationships with candidates as assets to be cultivated.

- If you pass the initial screening on the telephone and the evaluation of your resume, you will meet with the search consultant to determine whether you go onto the short list of candidates to be presented to the hiring organization.

CHAPTER 3

Making Yourself Visible to the Search Community

You'll recall that the staff at most search firms includes researchers as well as search consultants. You want those researchers and consultants to know how to find you. In this chapter, we look at tools and tactics you can use to bring yourself to their attention—and how to handle the initial phone call from a search professional.

If a researcher phones you and determines that you are qualified for—and interested in—the position, he will pass your name on to a search consultant, who will call you within a few days. If you are already in the search firm's database and meet the position's general qualifications, the first call you receive may be from the consultant. In any event, you heighten the chances of receiving a call if you make sure that a few search firms are aware of you.

BASIC RESEARCH

Before making any phone calls, the search consultant and research staff design a strategy for the search. They review the briefing document and discuss the qualifications and location of the job and of potential candidates. The consultant and staff identify likely sources of superior candidates in industries, functional areas and specific companies—called "target companies"—which often include competitors. Also, they will identify possible "sources," people who they know are not suited to the position but who can help them network toward someone who is.

Researchers will then review the firm's database of potential candidates. They will browse the websites of target companies and other online sources such as the BlueSteps® database (www.bluesteps.com), which is free to all search firms who are AESC members. Researchers will "cold-call" people they do not know but have identified from websites and other sources such as conference brochures, articles in the business press and directories from industry associations. Researchers also network among people they know from past searches, including executives they have previously placed, people in industry associations and even business journalists, industry analysts and other observers of the business scene.

This effort produces a "target list" of sources and prospects (the latter being potential candidates). A good number of these people have never been contacted by the search firm, only identified. Nor have they been evaluated for the position; this initial screening only places them on the target list, which directs the search toward the most promising avenues. This initial targeting also provides your entry point into the search process, because *you must be identified as a potential candidate before you can be evaluated as one.*

SOURCE OR PROSPECT?

If you are contacted by a search professional, that means you have been identified as a possible source or prospect. When a researcher calls, you may wonder which of the two you are.

A source is someone the search firm contacts to gather names of executives who might be suitable for the position. Then the researcher or consultant calls those executives and either finds that they are indeed potential candidates or continues networking toward such candidates. If you are a source, the researcher may start by saying something to the effect of, "I'm calling from an executive search firm about a position that we are retained to fill. It may possibly be of interest to you, but if not, then perhaps you will know others for whom it may be a fit." The researcher will then briefly describe the position (e.g., "senior vice president of marketing for a major consumer products company") and ask if you know of a potential candidate or additional source.

In contrast, a prospect is someone the search firm contacts as a potential candidate for the position. The researcher or consultant believes that a prospect possesses the broad qualifications for the position, and wants to evaluate that person's qualifications and interest in the opportunity.

Many times a source turns into a prospect. A recent AESC survey found that search firms reported this to be the case 23 percent of the time. In any event, a call from a search professional who views you as a source gives you an opportunity to establish a relationship with the firm. If you can provide names and contact information for one or more prospects, do so. At your request, the researcher or consultant will either use or not use your name when approaching these people. If you don't want your name used, be sure to say so.

We'll discuss how to handle initial phone calls later in this chapter, and in more depth in Chapter 4. Now let's look at how you can get your name onto these lists of sources and prospects.

GETTING NOTICED

You can become visible to the search community through two strategies: by increasing your visibility to the entire business community and by cultivating relationships with search professionals. We suggest that you pursue both. This amounts to something of a personal public relations program, which is not as difficult as it may sound. We're not talking about getting you on the cover of *Fortune* or *Business Week* although that would be nice. We're talking about your becoming known in your industry and profession (assuming that you've already achieved fame within your organization; if you haven't, start there).

What tactics can you use to raise your visibility? There are various avenues, assuming that you hold a true executive position. Here are seven proven ways to bring yourself to the attention of the executive search community:

- Join organizations

- Break into print

- Be accessible to search professionals

- Target recruiters and build relationships

- Keep an updated resume handy

- Be visible online

- Network, and then keep networking

Let's take each of these in turn:

Join Organizations

To become known in your profession, join your company's industry association and your professional organization. Your company no doubt belongs to a trade group or association. If it doesn't, have it join one; then become one of your company's representatives. There's an association for virtually every industry and functional area, be it marketing, finance, IT or HR. There are also associations for specialties within functions, such as direct-marketing professionals, corporate treasury managers and so on. Check the Web and, in your local library, hard-copy and CD-ROM directories of business and professional organizations.

But it's not enough to join a trade group or association; you also have to become active in it. Attend the regional, national and international meetings and conferences, and make the most of these networking opportunities. Better still, offer to serve on the conference program as a speaker, panelist or moderator, holding forth on your area of expertise. Simply being featured in the conference brochure generates positive exposure.

Also, volunteer for the next opening on a standing committee, such as the best-practices or ethics committee, or join one which plans and coordinates the association's conferences. Conference committees *always* want a helping hand. It's a great way to meet people who are heavily involved in the organization and in their industry. These are the people you want to know and be known to.

Break into Print

Take advantage of the past two decades' explosive growth in business publications and media coverage. When you are promoted, make sure it's announced in your industry's trade publications and the business section of your local newspaper. If you are instrumental in a (positive) story about your company and it is appropriate, work with journalists, through your corporate communications department, to get your name involved—without grabbing undue credit or upstaging your boss.

Write articles for your organization's newsletter or your industry's trade magazine. If you can land a column in a trade magazine for a period of time, so much the better. Regional business magazines and even city business newspapers are other promising outlets. These tactics may seem unrealistic to some readers, but others will know that there's nothing magical about it. Business publications constantly need features, news and information, and they are happy to get them from someone with expertise and authority.

Don't worry if you freeze up at the sight of a blank Word file or don't know a verb from an adverb. Trade magazines often lack good material and, unless you are masquerading as a freelance writer, they usually expect an executive to submit a rough draft. Their editors can edit your piece. If your company has a communications department, try to tap a ghostwriter there. Or perhaps you can simply serve as an interviewee or a quote source. Absent that, towering stacks of books have been published on how to approach editors and get yourself into print.

Be Accessible to Search Professionals

Believe it or not, there are executives who fend off phone calls from researchers and search consultants. Others treat them as if they were pesky salespeople. This doesn't exactly increase visibility in the search community. It's also counter to executives' interests. After all, a search professional is typically calling on the basis of research that indicates the prospect may be qualified for greater responsibilities.

Why would anyone avoid such phone calls?

Some executives seem to believe that talking to a recruiter is disloyal to their current employer. Others think that the conversation will be discovered and that they will be escorted out of the building by the security staff. In fact, it's quite likely that their superiors regularly speak with recruiters and almost certainly employ them. More to the point, that loyal executive would be promptly laid off or terminated if the company's financial situation dictated it. Few people sentimentalize their employers anymore, but if you do, please consider the idea that you may owe yourself and your dependents even more loyalty than you do your employer. Dealing with a search professional is a business situation, just like dealing with an employer.

A retained search consultant will respect your confidentiality and time. If you prefer, he will call you at home during off-hours. He will not pressure you to divulge information or pursue an opportunity against your wishes. He will not submit your resume to anyone without your permission. Some search consultants may seem a bit crisp in their manner at first, but that's a matter of personal style, which invariably softens as the relationship progresses. So don't be put off on that account.

Everything we suggest in this book assumes that you are at least willing to converse with executive search consultants once you know that they are legitimate (more on this in Chapter 4). In fact, simply returning calls from search firms can put you on their radar screens: An AESC study found that 46 percent of surveyed researchers reported that not having calls returned was their greatest frustration. Also, be sure your administrative assistant or receptionist knows that you accept calls from people you don't know (though you may still want to instruct that certain people should be screened out). The same study found that 40 percent of researchers cited aggressive gatekeepers as a major barrier to contacting potential candidates.

For obvious reasons, a search professional often won't identify himself as a recruiter or name his firm in a message left with a third party. Most will simply leave a name and phone number and say that they're calling regarding "personal business" or working on a "consulting assignment" or "research." Today, however, most executives can have calls put through to private voice-mail boxes. Instruct your administrative assistant to direct calls of this nature to that mailbox. Then return those calls. You'll have to ignore or shake off the occasional unwanted call, but you will at least know when you are being considered for a potentially better position.

Target Recruiters and Build Relationships

Target specific recruiters and build relationships with them *before you need a new position*. Search consultants typically approach people who are already employed, so approach them when you hold that status. (This is not to say that a search consultant won't present a qualified but unemployed candidate.)

As mentioned in Chapter 1, search consultants specialize along industry or functional lines, or sometimes both. (Most cover several specialties.) It therefore makes sense to target a small number of search firms—and specific consultants—that you want to know about you. You can identify retained executive search firms, as well as individual search consultants, by visiting the firms' websites, which you can access through links at www.aesc.org. In addition, use *SearchConnect*, the interactive membership directory of the AESC, which lists all member firms and their consultants by geographical location, function and industry at www.aesc.org or via www.bluesteps.com.

You can simply cold-call or e-mail a search consultant who covers your beat. While it's preferable to be approached by or referred to search consultants, most of them will listen to any competent executive—up to a point. Keep it brief and say that you understand his areas of specialization cover your field of experience, and that you would welcome a few moments to talk about market opportunities.

Although many search assignments are confidential, some firms post those that are not onto a section of their websites. It can be worthwhile to check the sites of your targeted firms to see if new positions have been posted. Apply only for positions for which you are suited or you will damage your credibility and squander your time. Also, remember that if you are in the firm's database or the BlueSteps® database, search consultants can find you when they have a position to discuss.

When a recruiter calls, first establish their legitimacy. Once you are satisfied, be friendly and frank about your background. Don't be afraid to sell yourself in an intelligent way. For instance, when you talk about your experience, mention accomplishments that benefited your organization. If you are multilingual or have any special skills or a desire to relocate (especially overseas), mention that as well. If you come across as friendly and helpful as well as successful, you'll probably hear from the search consultant again. If you were the consultant, whom would you call? Someone friendly and helpful, or someone else? Over time, you and the consultant will become more comfortable with one another. If the consultant is on a search to fill a position that you're qualified for, you may well be the first person called.

Have an Updated Resume or Curriculum Vitae (CV)

This may seem basic, and it is. Yet, as you know, success comes partly through diligent execution of the basics. Here are a few Dos and Don'ts:

Do:

- Clearly state your employers, titles and functional responsibilities, such as finance, marketing and so on. This will help researchers retrieve your resume when they search their databases for matches on those key words.

- Use strong verbs and phrases such as "led," "achieved," and "produced."

- Highlight one or two *major* accomplishments with each employer. Mention dollar figures, percentages or growth rates whenever you can ("reduced costs by $8 million" or "tripled division revenue in four years").

- Send your resume or CV, with a cover letter, to selected databases and search firms.

Don't:

- Overwhelm readers with long lists of bullets under each employer.

- Take more than two pages (unless it's a convention in your industry, as it is in academe).

- Use weak wording such as "oversaw," "was involved in" or "assisted in."

- Put off updating your resume or CV. Telling a search consultant that you "need a few days to put together a resume" is not the mark of an energetic careerist.

Have a brief verbal summary of your experience in mind and consider rehearsing it to yourself. You should be able to deliver these career highlights, talking at a reasonable pace, in about a minute. Be prepared to expand on any point that you make in this summary, if asked to do so.

Most people tend to load a resume or verbal summary with too many details. That's too bad because the impressive facts get buried among the trivial ones. Choose your real accomplishments and let them stand on their own, where anyone reviewing your background will see them.

Be Visible Online

The Web and various databases have become key research tools in executive search, as they have in every area of business. Search firms maintain internal databases of people their consultants have contacted or interviewed. Some firms maintain files of unsolicited resumes, which may or may not be integrated into their main database.

Search firms may also access external databases in the process of developing their lists of sources and prospects. The use of these databases—which might include university, industry, corporate and association resources—depends on the search and on the firm's experience with those resources. If your alumni, industry and professional associations maintain databases of biographical or professional information, consider listing yours. (Be sure to check the accuracy of your information before you submit it *and* after it's posted on the site.) Browse your alma mater's website and take advantage of any useful career management tools you find there. Also, be sure that you are represented on your company's website, assuming that your position warrants a spot, and, if there is one, in the company's online directory.

In all cases, submit your resume, biography and background only to sites that have credibility (generally these are the "official" sites of recognized institutions) and that respect confidentiality. Sites that broadcast or sell your name or information will in all likelihood generate more annoyance than opportunity.

Network, Then Keep Networking

Earlier we said that information (along with integrity) represents a search consultant's stock-in-trade. For that reason, a consultant spends a good portion of the week networking. Talking to people. Listening to people. Bartering information. Gathering facts—about the job market, companies and their plans, individuals and their careers and so on—for current searches and future reference.

We suggest that you do the same. You need not network with the vigor of a search consultant, but enough to know what's going on in your industry. Also, network enough so that colleagues and contacts think of you when they hear from a search professional. People, even some you barely know, will develop an awareness of you when you take a genuine interest in them and their needs. This idea strikes some people as idealistic or, perhaps, impractical. However, networking can be done in two basic ways: either "What can you do for me?" or "What can I do for you?"

Which approach do you think works better? Which approach does more to increase *your* awareness of someone else? Most of us remember people who help us, especially if they went out of their way to do so. So when you take a call from a researcher or search consultant or meet people at a trade association (or a civic or charitable organization—virtually all senior executives belong to *at least* one), think about what you can do for them. If you develop this habit, you will be surprised at the number of people you can help, and who will help you.

WHAT WORKS BEST?

Everything! All of these tactics for gaining visibility work. By that we mean that no single tactic will necessarily work on its own, but together they will. Like a corporate public relations program, a personal PR program succeeds on accumulated mentions and appearances over time. Repeated impressions generate name recognition. So use at least a few of these approaches, and don't expect instant results. One article or two appearances at conferences will not put your name on everyone's lips. The more of these tactics you use and the longer you use them, the more they will reinforce one another by bringing you to the attention of various people in various ways.

WHAT'S NEXT?

If you have used the foregoing tactics, have a record of achievement and have advanced to a senior-management level (or one level below), you will eventually receive a call from a researcher or a search consultant. You may even be targeted by the hiring organization as one of the potential candidates that the consultant absolutely must contact about the position.

However it originates, this could be one of the most important calls—perhaps *the* most important call—of your career. In the next chapter, you'll learn how to prepare for it and for the events that will follow.

ACTION POINTS

- To become a candidate in an executive search, you must first be identified by a search firm and then be evaluated as a suitable candidate. Fortunately, there are specific tactics you can use to increase your visibility to search professionals.

- To make yourself more visible to the search community, make yourself more visible to the business community. Do this by becoming active in organizations, getting your name in print and networking vigorously. You can also establish a relationship with a search consultant by contacting a few who work in your industry or discipline.

- Be accessible to search firms by taking—and returning—phone calls from search professionals. This alone will position you to make connections that many executives simply pass up.

- If you have not already done so, register your resume with the AESC's www.bluesteps.com. Use easy-to-access keywords to heighten your resume's chances of retrieval in database searches.

- Keep a resume or CV, and rehearse a brief verbal summary of your background and experi-

ence so you are prepared when a search professional calls.

• Think of drawing the attention of search professionals as a long-term project and as part
of a larger strategy to gain visibility in your
industry and profession. The tactics in this
chapter will work *if* you use a few of them
consistently over time.

CHAPTER 4

When Opportunity Knocks

When you receive a phone call from a search firm, either a researcher or a search consultant will be on the other end of the line. As you know from Chapter 3, he will be contacting you either as a source or a prospect, but remember that sources often morph into prospects.

In this chapter we show you how to handle that initial phone call and subsequent calls, which lead to interviews first with the search consultant and then with the hiring organization.

OPENING LINES

Researchers and consultants all have their individual approaches, but generally they open the initial telephone conversation with some version of:

> *"Hello, I'm Steve Smith calling from Quest Associates International. We're an executive search firm that has been retained by a _____ ___ [global financial institution, European food processor, etc.] to assist them in hiring a chief financial officer for a $350 million division of theirs."*

At this point *do not* ask, "How did you get my name?" It wastes time and usually elicits a vague answer. If it's germane, the consultant will volunteer that information. The question also smacks of mild paranoia. Worse, it may imply that you perceive yourself to be so insignificant that you're astonished that news of your existence would reach the ear of a search consultant.

Instead, simply indicate your willingness to have a brief conversation. But first ascertain who is calling you. Ask if the consultant is working on a *retained* search. At a minimum, you want to know whether the caller is working on a specific assignment or simply fishing for candidates or resumes.

Ask for the name and location of the search firm and, if it is not familiar to you, quickly check their website for information, or ask the consultant to send a brochure. Also check www.aesc.org to learn if it is a member of the AESC, which is the professional association of retained executive search firms. If the firm is a member, it has been vetted for professional practices and reputation and recognizes the *Candidate's Bill of Rights* (see Appendix).

Now, back to the conversation: The caller may throw in a detail or two about the location of the job, the amount or type of experience or any special skills required, such as a specific language. Then he will ask:

> *"Would you be interested in learning more about this opportunity?"*

At this point you must decide whether you possess the broad qualifications for the position and if you have any interest in pursuing it. If you're not sure, one sensible response would be to say, "I'd like to hear a bit more about the position." That buys you a moment to think, and you may hear another detail or two. The consultant may give you the name of the client or may not, even if you ask. Many search consultants, as a matter of discretion, won't name the client until they know they have a qualified, interested candidate on the line.

In any event, the consultant will soon say:

"Tell me a bit about yourself."

Here is where the brief verbal summary of your background mentioned in Chapter 3 comes in handy. Deliver it in a friendly, matter-of-fact manner and then stop talking. Do not ramble on or go into great detail. Armed with the briefing document and their experience, search professionals can quickly size someone up as a potential candidate.

If you are not a potential candidate, the caller will let you know in polite terms, saying, for example, "I don't think this position would be quite right for you." If you still believe you should be considered, you can say so and mention your reasons, which may or may not make a difference. If not, accept that fact. Then, assuming that the caller has come across as a professional, you should pursue a relationship. Offer names of potential sources or prospects or offer to call back in a day or two after thinking about who might be of interest. Ask the caller for his phone number, thank him for calling and tell him that you would be interested in hearing about future positions and in helping out on a search if you can.

The caller may ask you to suggest potential candidates or help him understand the structure of a certain company. You may initially feel imposed upon, but keep in mind that relationships are built on shared information and experiences, and you are trying to establish a relationship with the search consultant. You should, of course, reserve all confidential or sensitive information about your company and other people. But it pays to be helpful, and you may benefit a colleague. Again, be sure to get the caller's name and contact information.

If you are considered a potential candidate, it's imperative that you handle this initial call well. Even if you are not ultimately referred to the client organization, you still have an excellent opportunity to start a relationship with a search firm.

BECOMING A CANDIDATE

As noted, to become a candidate you must be interested in, and qualified for, the position. If you express interest in the position at this time, then the search consultant will assume your continued interest in the position. But consider any non-compete or employment contracts that you have signed. Some contracts have provisions that may preclude or limit your job mobility. If that's the case, say so right away to avoid wasted time or mistaken impressions.

Before meeting in person, the consultant will want to obtain some information regarding your qualifications and then decide whether you are a definite—as opposed to potential—candidate for the position. Answer all questions (that is, those that you feel comfortable answering) truthfully. After you supply this additional information, do not be surprised or disappointed if the consultant tells you that the position is not appropriate for you. That is the most common outcome. The consultant knows far more about the job and the client company than you do and is therefore in a better position to determine whether you would be a good fit.

At this point the search consultant's assessment involves the following four issues, and you can expect talking points and questions along these lines:

Issue #1: Are you at the right level for the position?

- Tell me about your current position and the department or functions that you manage.

- How does your department fit into the organizational structure? To whom do you report?

- How many people report to you? What key positions report to you? What do the people who report to you do?

- What are the company's annual revenues? How large is your department in terms of revenue or budget?

Issue #2: Do you have the right kind of experience for the position?

- Give me a brief chronology of your career: education, employers, key positions and compensation history.

- Tell me about the different roles you have had in your career. Which roles have you most enjoyed?

- Were any of these positions held outside your country of citizenship?

- What do you consider the major accomplishments in your career? To what do you attribute those successes?

Issue #3: Can the client offer you competitive compensation?

- What is your current compensation range?

- What is your base salary, and what is your potential (and actual) bonus and other incentive compensation?

- When was the most recent increase in your compensation? When do you expect your next increase?

Issue #4: How interested are you in considering a new position?

- How long have you been with your current company? How do you feel about your current responsibilities, compensation and pace of advancement?

- At what type of company and in what role would you most like to work?

- Have you considered a career change recently? Are you willing to relocate? Travel?

- What are the terms of your current employment? Do you have an employment contract? If so, when does it come up for renewal?

- Would you be interested in learning more about this opportunity?

You probably won't have to field all of these questions in the initial telephone conversation. At this stage, you and the search consultant are getting to know each other. Of course, from his standpoint the consultant has a binary decision to make: He either adds you to the list of candidates or screens you out. Again, being screened out is not a bad thing. You have lost nothing. In exchange for spending 15 or 20 minutes chatting on the phone, you have made a new, possibly valuable contact.

If your answers to questions like those above indicate that you fit the desired profile, and you have expressed interest in the position, you become a potential candidate. Be prepared to send a copy of your resume to the search firm. Also, request the website addresses for the search firm and the client. Ask for a copy of the briefing document for the position as well. Tell the consultant the best method and time to reach you, and ask about his preferred method of communication.

YOUR QUESTIONS

Of course you will have questions too. Typically, either before or after posing questions like those above, the consultant will tell you the name of the company and the position's title, location, reporting relationships, responsibilities and compensation. While the consultant wants to determine whether or not you're a potential candidate, he also wants the job to sound attractive. After all, if you're qualified, he'll want you to pursue the position.

If the recruiter reserves the name of the company, or other details you would like to know, ask why. The search, or certain details about the position, may be confidential. Or he may simply be holding back some information, such as who would interview you, until you need to know it or until it is likely to pique your interest. In any event, if you ask for information you are expressing interest, and that may prompt him to reveal more.

You might ask about reporting relationships above and below the position, about whether this is a newly-created or vacated position (and if the latter, how long it's been vacant) and about its overall responsibilities. Be sure to ask about the timeline of the search. How soon can you expect to hear whether you are a candidate? If you are, when will you meet with the search consultant? If geographical location is an issue, where will you meet?

WHAT IF YOU'RE NOT INTERESTED?

If, after learning more about the opportunity, you are not interested in it, say so. There's no point in wasting the consultant's time (and yours). However, by way of building a relationship, you should provide any leads to other candidates or sources that you can.

THE STATE OF THE SEARCH

From the consultant's standpoint, a search is something of a "numbers game" in which they cast a fairly wide net at the beginning of the assignment, and then selectively winnow out prospects and candidates. On a typical search engagement, 34 percent of AESC member firms reported that they contact more than 70 people by telephone. As the search progresses, the consultant creates a list of the actual candidates that the search firm will present in the form of resumes and written impressions. The consultant will also conduct in-depth, in-person interviews with candidates. Those who make that cut go on the "short list" of candidates who will interview with the client company.

After you have been initially contacted, you should hear from the search consultant in seven to ten business days if he wishes to pursue matters with you. During that interval, the search firm may check your background and references as well as those of other candidates. (More on this in Chapter 5.) Often this will occur after you meet with the consultant, but before you interview with the client. You can use this time to learn a bit more about the search firm and the company. Until you hear that you will be meeting with the consultant, you need not invest too much time in preparation. However, be ready to move quickly. If the search is urgent—and many are—the consultant and the client may want to meet with you very soon after deciding that you are a desirable candidate.

If you don't hear back from the search consultant in seven to ten business days, call and ask for an update on your status. If you do not make the next cut, ask for feedback. You may not get a frank answer unless you press for one, and even then you may not. Search consultants tend to be diplomatic about such matters, and they are not in the career coaching business. You might ask if there were any specific holes in your experience that you should fill.

Be sure to end the interchange on a positive note: Thank the search consultant for his time and consideration, and tell him that you would be interested in hearing about any positions that he believes might be a fit. Mention, too, that you would be happy to help out as a source on any future searches in your industry or functional area.

INTERVIEWS AHEAD

If, on the basis of the telephone conversation and your resume, the search consultant considers you an actual candidate, interviews will be the next step. First you will meet with the consultant and, if you pass muster, then with the hiring organization. In the next chapter you'll learn what to expect in these interviews, and how to handle them.

ACTION POINTS

- When a search professional phones you, ask the name of the search firm and check their website or www.aesc.org for more information.

- If you are contacted as a source or as a prospect who turns out not to be a candidate, you still have an excellent opportunity to establish a relationship with the search consultant.

- In the initial phone call the researcher or consultant wants to determine whether you are a potential candidate based on your qualifications and interest in the position.

- If you are a potential candidate, either in the first or second call the search consultant will determine whether you are truly a candidate. Toward that end, he will ask questions about your level of responsibility, experience, compensation and interest. You should also ask questions about the hiring organization, position, reporting lines, responsibilities and compensation.

- If you pass this level of screening, the consultant will request a resume or CV. The subsequent step, which he may suggest at this point, would be for you and the consultant to meet for an interview.

CHAPTER 5

An Insider View of the Interview

At this point you have been judged by the search consultant to have the broad qualifications for the position. Yet the most crucial parts of the process—the interviews—lie ahead. No matter how good your qualifications are, you must perform well in the upcoming interviews in order to receive an offer.

Interviewing in the context of an executive search involves two stages: first, the search consultant will interview you, then, if that interview is a success, you will progress to several interviews with the client organization. In this chapter we focus on how to prepare for and handle these interviews.

THE SEARCH FIRM INTERVIEW

The interview with the search consultant might appear to be a more casual, lower-stakes situation than the interviews with the client. Yet the way you handle this interview determines whether you will meet the client. It will also determine whether the search consultant views you as a viable candidate for future positions, in the event that you are not placed on the current assignment. That's a real consideration, because at this stage you are probably one of six to eight candidates for the position. Three to six candidates will typically be referred to the client for interviews, and only one will receive an offer. If the lead candidate turns down the offer, that offer or a similar one is normally extended to the next candidate.

The consultant may want to interview you in his office, but possibly not. Often, logistics or a desire for a neutral environment will result in a meeting over breakfast, lunch or dinner. A search consultant coming from out of town may hold successive interviews in a hotel room or rented conference room. In that situation, the consultant cannot hold all interviews over meals, although some do schedule back-to-back lunches. (Light lunches, of course.)

Wherever the interview occurs, the consultant has two objectives: to determine whether your experience and qualifications truly match the requirements of the position, and to determine whether your personality and style will fit the organizational culture.

PREPARING FOR THE INTERVIEWS

To prepare for both search firm and client interviews, first review the briefing document. Focus on the specific qualifications and experience needed for the position. For example, the client may be seeking someone with international marketing experience. In that case you would write down all the positions you have had and evaluate each one for your involvement with international marketing. As noted, be as specific as you can in terms of your accomplishments, quantifying any increases in revenue, profit or market share. Be sure to consider any special projects, task forces or committees you have served on or headed.

Before the search firm interview, learn enough about the organization to be able to ask about the company's strategy, situation and plans. Know what's on the organization's website and what's been written in the business press over the past year or so. If the company's stock is publicly traded, read its most recent annual report to shareholders and understand its financial condition.

Prepare good questions about the position. Is it in an area that has been growing, contracting or flat? Whatever the case, what is management's strategy? Is the client seeking someone to capitalize on an opportunity or to polish a lackluster operation? What is the upside potential and downside risk of the position? The consultant's answers to these questions—those that he can answer—will help you frame further questions for the client. In all interviews, ask questions in a positive, open manner. Never appear to be negative or suspicious. Speak matter-of-factly to show that you understand business has its ups and downs and that you want to be prepared for both.

Also, anticipate the likely questions that you will be asked—samples of which follow—and prepare yourself to deliver your answers naturally:

- What do you consider your major career accomplishments?

- Why are you interested in this position and this organization?

- Why would you consider leaving your current employer?

- Where do you see yourself in three, five and ten years?

- What specific short-term contributions do you feel you could make to this organization?

- Give an example of a challenge or problem you faced and how you dealt with it. Give another example.

- What do you consider your strengths and weaknesses?

In all cases be as factual as you can and be positive. Avoid self-deprecating remarks but be honest and forthcoming. This will be appreciated by the search consultant—remember, nobody is perfect.

Finally, be sure to bring up any concerns prompted by your research. If sales or profits have been flat or falling, if the company has been selling divisions or the stock has taken a beating, ask the search consultant about it. If you don't want these concerns mentioned to the company, say so. But, again, raise your concerns in a matter-of-fact manner.

CONSIDER YOUR IMAGE

Like the earlier discussion of resumes, this section may seem basic to you, but dress and grooming greatly affect the impression you will make. The strategy of dressing for the job you want has been around for a long time, and is still terrific advice for interviewees for senior executive positions. The search consultant and the client don't know you. Therefore, they will inevitably base their initial opinion of you mainly on your appearance and your way of expressing yourself.

Whereas most clients prefer candidates for executive positions to take a conservative approach to dress and self-expression, some industries, notably advertising and entertainment, not only tolerate but welcome executives with a more creative image. Many (but not all) executives in those industries wear trendy clothing and sprinkle their conversations with hip expressions, and like to be around people who do the same. But in most industries, clients want their organizations helmed by men and women in conservative suits, sensible shoes and conventional hairstyles. They are also reassured when candidates mention mainstream pastimes and vacation spots.

That said, be yourself and things will work out for the best. If you are creative and trendy, you probably won't be recruited to head the investment function at a major insurance company. Similarly, if you favor pinstriped suits and don't know rap from hip-hop, you probably haven't been asked to head up a new division of a music TV channel. Search consultants are adept at matching candidates to organizations, so when you interview with the client, maintain the persona you presented to the consultant.

FOUR TYPES OF INTERVIEWS

Both search consultants and hiring organizations might employ any of the four basic types of employment interviews: the behavioral-based, conversational, panel or stress interview, or some combination of two or more. Here's what to expect in each type of interview:

Behavioral-Based Interview

In the behavioral-based interview, the interviewer asks questions in a specific order to give you the opportunity to demonstrate certain behaviors and personality attributes. Quite often these questions are phrased along the following lines: "Give me an example of a time when you performed under pressure."

Your answer to that question should demonstrate how you respond to pressure. So rather than saying, "I generally handle pressure well," describe specific decisions and actions that you have taken in response to pressure. You might also describe a specific approach that you use in difficult situations—such as Ask, Analyze and Act—and then give an example of how you applied that approach. From the examples you cite, the interviewer tries to gauge whether you have the skills to perform in the position.

Conversational Interview

A conversational interview is what it sounds like—an interview framed as a conversation. This is the most common type of interview. Some people who use the conversational interview are either unprepared or judge you mainly on chemistry or how you come across. However, most interviewers who use this approach have specific questions they want answered. The more skillful ones will jump around from topic to topic, sometimes circling back to see if you give consistent answers or add depth or examples to earlier answers. Be prepared to do so.

Don't let the less formal tone of this type of interview lead you to believe that it is a casual conversation. It isn't. The interviewer is judging you as much as he would in any other mode of interview. So don't relax too much. Stay focused and use the same tone the interviewer uses. Answer all questions completely and with specific examples. Also, if the interviewer asks for your career or life history, he is handing you a long length of rope. Make sure you don't hang yourself with it by becoming so fascinated with your early achievements that you leave little time to cover your more recent experience relative to the current opening. Summarize the early part of your career in an organized, fast-paced way and then bring your more recent achievements to the fore.

Panel Interview

As the name implies, in the panel interview you simultaneously face two or more interviewers. If you doubt your memory, take a moment to write the interviewers' names and titles on a pad in "seating chart" fashion. Maintain eye contact mainly with the person who asked you the question, but include the others in your reply as well.

Stress Interview

The stress interview is the most difficult type. The interviewer may ask rapid-fire questions, display a brusque manner or even challenge you somehow. Your first reaction might be irritability or anger. Neither of those responses will win you points. You will only appear to be easily rattled, which is exactly what you want to avoid.

To handle the stress interview, first realize that the interviewer doesn't know you, so there's no reason to take his aggressive manner personally. Second, understand that you are being tested on how you deal with stress, pressure and unpredictability. Third, remain calm and answer the questions directly, as you would in a behavioral-based or conversational interview. If the interviewer rushes you, repeat the question back to him to buy some time to develop your answer.

In AESC's recent survey, 49 percent of search firms reported that they use the conversational approach to interviewing candidates, 34 percent said they use a combination of methods. So be ready for anything they throw at you.

AT THE HIRING ORGANIZATION

Before interviewing with the client, talk with the consultant about what to expect. You might even ask for some interview "prep time" on the phone. While search consultants are not job-search coaches, they're intimately familiar with the interview process. Moreover, the consultant has interviewed you and wants to see you successfully complete your subsequent interviews. By requesting help, you're telling the consultant that you're seriously pursuing the position and that you value his expertise and opinion. Most search consultants will assist you.

Speaking of seriously pursuing the position, we suggest that you do exactly that. Never go into an interview just to see what you're worth in the market. This isn't a fishing expedition. In the first place, that would not be an honest way to treat the search consultant or the client, both of whom take your expressions of interest as sincere. Second, you would be wasting everyone's time, including yours.

So the goal is to get an offer. This is not to say that you must accept it. In fact, if you learn during the interviews that the position or company is not for you, then you should withdraw from the process. However, the objective in an interview is to present yourself in the most positive light. The people interviewing you will also be presenting themselves and the position that way. If you enter an interview in a half-hearted spirit, your lack of commitment will show. So go in with the objective of learning all you can and letting the interviewers learn about you. That way, everyone can see if your fit with the position represents an opportunity for all concerned.

Before the Interview

Learn the titles, responsibilities and names (and pronunciation of names) of the interviewers. Ask the search consultant about the interviewers' personal styles. If a particular interviewer tends to be unusually quiet and passive or boisterous and aggressive, it's good to know that up front.

Attend to other details as well: Have the time and place of the interviews written down, along with clear directions and the interviewers' phone number. Leave plenty of time to get there. (Failure to plan for something as predictable as a traffic jam may indicate lack of foresight on your part.) Be familiar with the company's major lines of business, products and recent strategic moves such as mergers, acquisitions, spin-offs, divestitures, and stock offerings or buy-backs. Finally, know the names of the most senior executives at the company or division to which you are applying. That way, if the interviewer refers to "Bob," you'll know that Bob is the CEO. Knowing such details shows that you're interested.

At the Interview

Remember all the basics. Firm handshake but no knuckle-crushing. Look people in the eye but don't stare. Answer the question with specific details, and don't ramble. If you don't know the answer or can't answer a question for some other reason, simply say so. If you feel the interview is going badly, do not communicate that. Try to steer the conversation into an area in which you feel more comfortable or back to an area where the interviewer seemed comfortable. Also, you may feel things are going badly when in fact they are not. You are meeting people under special circumstances, not at a social occasion, and your perceptions may be affected by those circumstances.

After the Interview

Write a thank-you note to the lead interviewer and ask him to extend your thanks to the others, whom you should name. Call the search consultant, thank him and ask what he heard from the client about the way things went. You may not hear immediate feedback, but within a week the consultant will be able to tell you whether an offer—or another round of interviews—is forthcoming. If you ultimately do not get an offer, thank the consultant for his efforts on your behalf, chalk it up as a useful experience and remain in touch with the consultant.

REFERENCES AND BACKGROUND CHECKING

If you are to be considered for an offer, the consultant and the hiring organization will need to check references and perform a background check. It is helpful for you to know what will be expected and what the process involves.

First and foremost, reference and background checking are not the same thing. References are subjective assessments gathered from others to help the consultant and employer assess whether you are as good as they think you are and therefore suitable for the position, while background checking researches your credentials and career history.

Reference checking involves subjective assessment of comments and opinion from coworkers, superiors and even subordinates at your most recent jobs. How far back to go in your career and who to talk to are matters of judgment, and will be agreed between the consultant and the hiring organization. It is entirely likely that the future employer will take some of the references directly to satisfy himself about your attributes against the requirements of the job. Be aware that the risk in new employment exists on both sides, and the costs of getting it wrong for the employer can be very considerable. Due diligence in executive search is thus a key component of the service—don't be surprised if the process is extremely thorough.

The consultant will ask you for reference suggestions and will seek your permission as to who may be contacted and when. Consult with your references before giving their names to the search consultant. Inaccurate or incomplete reference checking may result in an unsatisfactory hire and cause damage to the consultant's reputation. Within the confines of relevance, probity and confidentiality, the search consultant may continue with further reference checking if he feels it to be necessary.

Formal background checking of your credentials and career history will also take place, and may be undertaken by the search firm itself, the future employer or by a third-party background checking firm hired by either the search firm or the employer.

It is important to recognize that such checking will occur. Therefore, do not conceal significant issues or events that could cause you severe embarrassment or even harm your career were they to become known later. These include: significant civil or criminal litigation; concealed appointments that you do not feel reflect well on your overall career; degrees or professional qualifications that you do not have. Minor oversights will be excused but a significant issue such as claiming a degree that was not earned, despite attendance at the college, are transgressions that will not be forgiven at the senior level and may well lead to dismissal. There is, unfortunately, an increasing amount of resume fraud today and search consultants and employers are much more sensitive to this possibility. It is just not worth the risk.

The timing of the references and background checks will depend upon the dynamics of the assignment. Generally speaking, since at the senior-management level references will need to be taken well before serious contract negotiations are entered into, references from your current employer may serve as a formality at the end of the process, rather than as a key part of the recruitment process. Overall, remember that it is *your* career and you should be consulted as to when and how the referencing will occur.

If your references work out well and you get an offer…well, that's the subject of the next chapter.

ACTION POINTS

- Realize that the objective in an employment interview is to obtain an offer. You want to learn all you can about the organization and position, but understand that you are selling yourself and must present yourself in the best light.

- Conduct thorough research and be well-prepared. Solid preparation will demonstrate your interest in the position, give you confidence and set you apart from other candidates.

- Ask the search consultant for some interview prep time on the phone. Learn all you can beforehand about the people you will be interviewing and the schedule of your day.

- Be ready for any of the four types of interviews: the behavioral-based, conversational, panel or stress interview, or a combination.

- At all times in the interviews, remain calm and confident, answer questions directly, and if you don't know the answer to a question, simply say so.

- Be prepared for in-depth reference and background checking. Think through a list of relevant referees and consult them before giving their names to the search consultant.

CHAPTER 6

Responding to an Offer and Negotiating Compensation

If you are offered a position at the client organization, congratulations. You have survived a rigorous screening, recruiting, interviewing and decision-making process, against formidable competition. That fact gives you significant leverage. While you do not want to overplay your hand, you owe it to yourself to negotiate the best compensation package that you can.

In this chapter we explain the components of an offer, how to negotiate your compensation and how to go about leaving your current employer.

THE OFFER: WHEN AND WHAT

An offer usually, but not always, occurs in two stages: the offer of the position and the offer of the compensation. Sometimes these are delivered simultaneously. It is somewhat to your advantage if the position is offered first, because then the organization has said that they want to hire you, and you can say you accept the position—on condition that the compensation and other conditions of employment are satisfactory.

Although you will have discussed the salary parameters with the search consultant to ensure that they are generally satisfactory, you should not raise the issue of compensation with the hiring organization. It's the employer's place to do so, and you are in a better negotiating position if they have "first serve" and present an initial offer. If you are asked about your salary expectations before you are offered the position, be vague but positive. Say something like, "The important thing to me is the position, the organization and the contribution I could make. Given those, I'm sure we can work out the compensation."

Sometimes the organization will extend the offer through the search consultant. More often, the offer will come directly from a representative of the company. *Never* accept an offer on the spot. Regardless of the offer, say you will need a few days to consider it. Is that what you should say even if the offer exceeds your highest expectations? Yes!

Here's why: There are too many components in an executive compensation package for you to analyze and agree to on the spot—and once you agree, you are committed. Salary and bonus are only two elements of compensation. The main components, not all of which are part of every executive's compensation, might include:

- Base salary and usually a bonus based upon individual, departmental and/or company performance

- Profit sharing, particularly in small companies, partnerships, and professional and service firms such as law firms and ad agencies

- Stock options, which allow the holder to purchase the company's stock at a specific (usually below-market) price during a specific period

- Stock, such as restricted stock, which is an equity stake usually purchased at a specific time and price or given as part of compensation

- Signing bonus, a one-time payment offered either as an added incentive or to compensate for benefits being sacrificed on leaving your current employer

- Retirement benefits, which may include a company-funded pension and/or tax-deferred retirement-income plan to which both the company and employee contribute

- Paid or partially paid health insurance, dental insurance, disability insurance, life insurance and, often, long-term-care insurance

- Paid vacation

- Company car

- Relocation assistance

- Perquisites ("perks") such as use of the company plane or helicopter and company-paid or partially paid health club, country club, tuition for children and financial-planning assistance

Trends in executive compensation change frequently. For instance, "pay for performance" goes in and out of favor depending on whether or not it seems to be working. Compensation trends can also vary with changes in a nation's income tax policy. Speaking of which, be sure to consider the tax advantages or disadvantages of various forms of compensation, especially if you will be working in a country other than your own. For example, in the United States an equity stake may be worth more than cash compensation *if* the gains are taxed at the capital gains—rather than personal income tax—rate. Similarly, deferred compensation in the form of company contributions to a savings plan may see you through your sunset years more comfortably than equivalent savings from a higher current income, which may be subject to higher taxes.

Some components in the list above, such as the various types of insurance, may be standard at a given company and thus difficult or impossible to negotiate. The key, however, is to consider *all* of these items when you analyze your compensation, and then negotiate those that are both negotiable and important to you.

ABOUT NEGOTIATING

Few people, even among senior executives, enjoy negotiating, and most of us are not very good at it. The reasons involve cultural and psychological issues we need not go into here. But with preparation and a few rules of thumb, you can achieve a more favorable compensation package than you would without negotiating. That's because most large organizations have broad compensation policies and pay grades that they apply to employees at most levels—but not necessarily to senior management. These pay grades ensure that people in similar jobs are paid a similar average compensation. However, as a candidate recruited by a search firm, you have been judged to be superior not only to internal candidates but also to other candidates in the search. This means you should probably receive above-average compensation. In the executive ranks, even large companies with fairly rigid pay structures have at least some flexibility in crafting compensation packages. Smaller companies usually have even greater flexibility.

Some of this flexibility stems from the number of components in an executive compensation package. So a good starting point is to examine your specific needs and then learn whatever you can about compensation patterns at the organization. Explore the fit between your needs and the company's favored means of compensation. For example, to discourage turnover some companies provide excellent long-term benefits and somewhat lower current compensation. Some emphasize bonuses and other forms of incentive pay—such as profit sharing over straight salary—while others do the opposite. If you know about the organization's general approach, you will be better able to understand the offer and "speak their language" when you discuss your needs.

Regardless of how compensation is structured, the company's first offer will rarely be its best. Almost all companies leave room to increase the initial offer in case the candidate wants to negotiate higher compensation. By the same token, you should counter with a figure— for base salary and for total cash compensation—higher than the one you would expect. It will be much easier for you to agree to a lower figure than to bargain for a higher one.

The actual value of an executive to a company is extremely difficult to gauge. Compensation analysts have tried to tie executive pay to increases in revenue, profits, net worth, stock prices and so on. Yet there are no accepted formulas and very few guidelines. Therefore, in a market economy an executive's worth comes down to what an organization will pay. In other words, you get what you negotiate. Thus, it is your responsibility to understand your compensation package before you accept the position, and to get it in writing. This greatly reduces the possibility of disappointment or disagreement down the road.

THE ROLE OF THE SEARCH CONSULTANT

You should discuss the position's compensation range in your first or second conversation with the search consultant. There's no point in pursuing a position that's far above or below your current or past range.

As noted, the search consultant may convey the offer to you. Whether he does or the client does, the consultant will discuss the offer with you and either answer or get answers to any questions you may have about the package. He can help you understand the compensation package and perhaps explain the organization's posture regarding incentive pay, signing bonuses, etc. Include the search consultant in all compensation discussions. Although he works for the hiring organization, you can view him as an honest broker. He can help resolve issues, convey your views to the client and, if applicable, review the employment contract with you. (We discuss employment contracts below.)

However, the search consultant will *not* negotiate your compensation for you. A retained search firm's fee may be based on a percentage of the first year's cash compensation. If you negotiate higher compensation for yourself that may mean that the search firm's fee will increase (unless the retainer agreement states otherwise). But in order to maintain an ethical practice and avoid conflicts of interest, a search firm will not help a candidate negotiate higher compensation.

NEGOTIATING COMPENSATION 101

First, unless you have solid experience in negotiating compensation, don't go it alone. You need a sounding board and an adviser, and probably one that can support you more strongly than the search consultant can, given his relationship with the hiring organization. Your accountant, financial adviser or attorney, or a knowledgeable colleague may fill this role. But, if you are entering a very senior position either at a major company or a small privately held company, you might consult an executive-compensation specialist, who can advise or represent you in your negotiations. The fees of such experts can sometimes be negotiated as part of the compensation package. It is in the employer's interest that you have a satisfactory employment contract, since the alternative could create problems down the road.

Second, get the best information you can on the prevailing compensation for the position you're being offered. In any negotiating situation, the party with the best information has an advantage. Check out resources such as the websites of magazines for specific executive titles or functions, such as *CEO*, *CFO* and *CIO*, many of which publish annual salary surveys. Even if you must pay for a salary survey from one of the several firms that publish them, it's worthwhile to have good information. Compensation experts will also have access to this kind of information.

Third, consider your value from the standpoint of your current compensation and your value to the hiring organization:

- Calculate the *total* value of your current compensation and benefits, and of any payments you forgo by leaving your employer at this time. For example, if it is autumn and your new employer wants you onboard by year-end, you might not collect your annual bonus after the first of the year (depending on your employment contract). In such situations, consider requesting a signing bonus to cover or defray any losses you incur.

- Then consider your value to the hiring organization in the new position. How much more responsibility is involved? How much broader is the scope of the position? Will you have "P&L" responsibility—that is, responsibility for the profit and loss of a division or operating unit? Are the responsibilities different from those of your current position, or from the usual position of this type? Do the differences justify increased compensation?

Fourth, approach the negotiation with confidence. The organization has decided to hire you; only the terms need to be worked out. Don't strike an aggressive posture. Instead, take a calm approach and support your requests with reasons. If the employer counters your reasons and you cannot counter back, make a note of their rationale and think it over. Don't argue. Don't ask the company to do the impossible, such as providing an insurance or pension benefit unavailable to other senior managers. On the other hand, there should be flexibility on things like signing bonuses, relocation expenses and, of course, salary.

Finally, before and during the negotiations consider these Dos and Don'ts:

Do:

- Be certain the person you are negotiating with has the authority to decide the matters under discussion.

- Understand how much leverage you have, but don't overestimate. In general, the more unique your skills and the more they are needed, the greater your leverage. For instance, if a troubled company needs a president, a CEO with a record of successful turnarounds will have far more leverage than one without such experience.

- Define your "floor"—the minimum acceptable cash compensation in salary and bonuses and the benefits you must have—beforehand.

- Take notes during the discussions so you have a record of what was said and the steps to come.

- Phrase your wishes as requests rather than demands, and occasionally mention that you're enthusiastic about joining the organization.

- Ask for a review and a possible adjustment in six months—and get it in writing—if you can't negotiate your desired compensation.

- Get *everything* in writing when the compensation package is finalized, and review the document against the notes you took during negotiations.

Don't:

- Go into the negotiation believing that you must win on every issue; you'll probably win some and lose some.

- Fear rejection of your requests or approach the negotiation as if you are seeking a handout.

- Focus only on the short term to the detriment of your long-term career and finances.

- Nitpick by asking for small, potentially irritating concessions such as a car allowance that includes fuel, maintenance, washing and parking. Raising such requests during these delicate negotiations can lead an employer to second-guess your business judgment and, perhaps, the decision to hire you.

- Deliver ultimatums, become emotional or alienate your future boss or colleagues.

- Accept an offer without taking a day or so to think it over and discuss it with your adviser.

- Sign an employment contract without having your attorney or a knowledgeable colleague review it.

Another key point concerns the vesting of your rights in various benefits or plans. For example, when does your right to any deferred compensation, such as company contributions to a retirement plan, become irrevocably yours? Are you or your children eligible for tuition benefits immediately or only after you've been employed for some period? Regarding certain benefits, vesting periods and timing can be serious issues.

WHAT ABOUT AN EMPLOYMENT CONTRACT?

Although formal employment contracts involving a fixed term period and complex provisions on stock entitlements, etc., have become more common in recent years, they are still mostly applied only to chief executive positions or very senior management appointments. In most cases a senior executive will receive an employment letter which will provide for notice provisions on either side but not involve a fixed contractual term of office.

In the case of either a formal contract or an employment letter, however, the same basic principles apply. The document will define the employer-employee relationship and describe the responsibilities and duties, compensation and benefits, term of employment, conditions for termination, amount of severance pay and non-compete and non-disclosure provisions.

An employment contract or letter is a binding legal agreement, not a mere formality. Be sure you read and understand it, and that you and your employer sign it before you resign from your current position. Never view the deal as done until the employment contract has been executed. If you are told that it "may take a while to get out of the legal department," say that you must see the contract as soon as possible and that you can consider yourself employed only after it is executed.

As you know, the party that draws up a contract tends to favor itself. That's understandable. The company will protect its own interests, not yours. That's why you *must* have a clear understanding of your responsibilities and duties and the components of your compensation before the employment contract is finalized.

Key terms to review include:

- All components of your compensation package

- Responsibilities, duties and expectations of your position. A formal job description is fine but not necessary. However, do not accept a mere listing of your title, which is too open-ended for a legal document.

- Term of employment or of the contract, unless you are employed "at will," in which case either party can terminate whenever it wants to. If the contract expires, it should renew automatically.

- Conditions under which you can be terminated, for example "with cause" and with a definition of those causes (such as illegal actions)

- Severance pay or continuation of compensation *and* continuation of benefits for a defined period if you are terminated

- Language that prohibits you from disclosing trade secrets or from competing with your new employer within a certain period or geographical area (be cautious about these provisions, which can limit your ability to make a living if you are terminated or resign).

In this book we can only provide general guidelines and points to consider in an employment contract. Also, we are not attorneys and we cannot provide—nor are we providing—legal advice. As a rule, before signing any document created by an attorney, have the document reviewed by your attorney.

PARTING OF THE WAYS

When you have accepted the offer and have a start date and (if applicable) a signed contract, you are ready to resign your current position. You want to leave on good terms for the sake of your reputation and future references.

Have a formal letter of resignation to give to your employer when you deliver your verbal notice. Your employer will ask about your plans and may ask you to reconsider your decision. He may even ask for a chance to counter your new offer. Do not use this meeting to barter a new arrangement with your current employer. You have made the decision to leave the company and should hold to that decision because **A**) you made the decision in a well-reasoned manner **B**) your emotions may overwhelm your business judgment and **C**) you will not be viewed in the same way by your employer after announcing your resignation.

Make your resignation letter brief, businesslike and to the point, like the following sample:

```
Dear [insert name]:

This letter is to inform you of my
decision to resign from my position as
[insert title] at [insert company name]
as of [insert date].

Thank you for all the support you have
given me during my tenure here. I have
enjoyed working with you, and my decision
to leave was not made lightly. The new
position that I am moving into is, I
believe, an exciting opportunity to
further my professional and personal
goals.
```

```
I will make every effort to ensure that
my transition from the company is smooth,
and I look forward to assisting you in
any way I can during this period.

Sincerely,

[insert your name]
```

Provide enough notice to allow for a smooth transition, but realize that it is usually best to move on quickly. A lame-duck executive cannot get much done and is typically viewed as an obstacle by his successor. In addition, your new employer will be as eager to see you in your new role as you will be to enter it.

MAINTAIN CONTACT WITH THE SEARCH CONSULTANT

Don't forget to follow up with your search consultant once you have started work. Some search consultants will stay in touch with you for three to six months to make sure that your transition to the new position is a success, and he may be able to help sort out issues should they arise. You may also be able to offer help to the search consultant on other searches.

ACTION POINTS

- Recognize that when it comes to executive compensation you get what you negotiate. Most companies have at least some, and often considerable, leeway in the compensation they can offer to senior executives.

- Review your offer for all components in the compensation package, including benefits, deferred income and perquisites. Remember, if you are forgoing payments by leaving your current employer, you should ask your new employer to compensate you for that loss, perhaps with a signing bonus.

- Unless you have solid negotiating experience, get help from a knowledgeable adviser such as your accountant, financial planner, attorney or trusted colleague. Also, consider consulting a compensation expert, whose fees may even be paid by the employer. Include the search consultant in compensation discussions but understand that he cannot negotiate your compensation.

- Review any employment letter or contract carefully—and have your attorney review it— before you sign it. Pay special attention to the language in any non-compete or non-disclosure clauses, which may limit your ability to work in a certain industry or geographical area.

- Resign from your current employer in a professional, businesslike manner, and move to your new position as soon as you can while ensuring a smooth transition for your successor.

- Remain in touch with your search consultant as he can still be a source of guidance and help to you in the future. You may be able to help him as well.

C H A P T E R   7

Managing Your Senior Executive Career

Changes in employer-employee relationships over the past 25 years have transformed the modern corporation from something of a feudal state into more of an ever-changing professional team. The ability to meet increasingly ambitious goals has superseded seniority and loyal service as grounds for executive advancement. While some executives still spend their careers at one company where they rise through the ranks, they are the exception. Investors' demands for returns, fluctuating marketplace dynamics and activist boards and regulators have fostered enough turnover on "mahogany row" to give any executive pause. These trends are most pronounced in the United States, but are occurring even in nations such as Japan where companies once proudly provided "lifetime employment."

Many people see a lack of security in this state of affairs, and they are correct. Responsibility for your security has shifted from your employer to you. If the company won't "take care of you," then you must take care of yourself, which is the subject of this final chapter. Here we broaden our focus from handling yourself in an executive search to the larger issue of managing your entire career.

WHAT IS CAREER MANAGEMENT?

Career management encompasses everything you do to plan, finance, monitor and achieve professional advancement. You begin managing your career in an organization even before you join it. As the preceding chapters have shown, you must choose your employers wisely. You must only accept positions that offer the type of opportunities, challenges, risks and rewards that you desire. And you must negotiate the best possible deal for yourself. On the job, you must quickly decide where you can make the greatest contribution in light of your skills and responsibilities and the organization's needs and resources.

Managing at the senior level now demands true leadership skills. If you don't have them, you must develop them. You do not have to be a Franklin D. Roosevelt or Winston Churchill, but you must manage your subordinates with a view toward achieving the organization's goals. You also need to forge productive working relationships with subordinates as well as within the executive team. Focus on achieving results that measurably improve the organization's performance, preferably in terms of sales, profits and market share. This generally requires a combination of new initiatives and effective management of existing operations.

Be prepared for organizational politics. Politics arise from the ongoing "conversation" in every organization regarding proper goals and the best ways of achieving them. Effective executives bring facts and experience to that conversation. They try to manage on a factual basis, and certainly do so more consistently than those executives who are perceived as poor managers. Management based on facts, data and experience, rather than personalities and expediency, will ultimately prevail in most cases, but not in all. Companies in which the ongoing conversation is chaotic or excludes unpleasant facts are not good career bets, as bankruptcy records attest. If you find yourself in such a company, move on.

Career management also deals with matters beyond your current position and organization, and with what you want out of your professional and personal life.

KNOW THYSELF

To manage your career, you need an overall goal, interim objectives and plans for reaching both. Given that work consumes so much of our lives and can provide opportunities for stimulation, self-expression and fulfillment, it makes sense to start by knowing yourself. That knowledge will improve your chances of choosing work and organizations in which you will succeed.

So begin your career-management initiative with an inventory of your interests, attitudes, skills and desires. There are various ways of doing this. You can consult a career counselor, who, at your request or as a matter of course, might administer a standardized test such as the Strong Vocational Interest Inventory or the Myers-Briggs Type Indicator. These tests provide general indicators of your interests and personality traits. You can do various exercises on your own, such as imagining your ideal career or writing your own obituary (well in advance of the need, one hopes). You can also use the questions in the chart on the next page to examine your motivation.

As you conduct your inventory, be completely honest with yourself. It's easy for many people to make career choices based on what they think they should want,

Personal Motivation	Questions to Ask Yourself
Passion	What do you feel deeply about?
	What excites you?
	What would you do if you didn't have to work for a living?
	Can you make a career, and a living, out of your passion?
Nature	Are you a leader, follower, originator, executor, builder or maintainer?
	Do you work better with structured or less structured problems and environments?
	Do you prefer a large or small organization?
	Are you risk-averse or a risk taker?
	Are these traits reflected in your career so far and your plans for the future?
Desire	Do you truly enjoy a leadership role?
	Do you have a yearning to be in control and manage others, or would you rather work on your own?
	Do you enjoy (or at least respond well to) the pressures of organizational responsibility and accountability?
Skills	What are your current skills (e.g., finance, marketing, selling, analysis, planning, creating, writing, public speaking)?
	What skills do you most enjoy using?
	How would you rate your leadership skills?
	What skills would you like to have?

Personal Motivation	Questions to Ask Yourself
Self-improvement	What are you doing to improve your knowledge and skills? How will you acquire the experience necessary to achieve your long-term goal, for example to become a CEO? What experience, responsibilities and personal qualities will make you a candidate? (What "pieces" do you still need?)
Legacy	How do you want to be remembered? What sorts of things, both tangible and intangible, do you want to leave behind?

rather than what they really want. They choose careers they are unsuited to because they see them as acceptable, prestigious or lucrative. This undermines their prospects for success. Success in a career, including financial success, demands an investment of one's self. To be "fully invested" you must believe in what you're doing. If you don't, you will be at a serious disadvantage compared with people in your field who do believe in what they're doing.

Regardless of how you conduct your self-inventory, do it in writing. Writing forces you to think and express yourself more objectively and clearly than random musings will. Your career plan must also be in writing for the same reasons, and so you can refer to it and periodically gauge your progress.

YOUR CAREER PLAN

A survey taken some years ago found that most people spend more time planning their annual vacation than they do planning their career. That's a sterling example of misplaced priorities. In fairness, though, most people know more about vacation planning than they do about career planning. To make the subject manageable, let's break your career plan down into four parts—Goals, Preparation, Action, and Assessment/Adjustment—and examine each part.

Goals: Make Them Clear and Ambitious

In setting career goals, first set a time horizon. Your ultimate goal may be to leave a certain legacy. If that's too cosmic (or morbid) for you, then think about retirement. Or consider a time frame to move into a second career as an entrepreneur, teacher or scholar. Think about professional *and* financial goals one, two, three, five and ten years into the future—and longer. Many executives key their five, ten and twenty year-goals—and their retirement—to certain birthdays or calendar years, typically those ending in five or zero. Also, set goals for yourself at each organization you join and for each position you assume.

Any of the following would constitute reasonable goals:

- To become independently wealthy and retire by age 50

- To achieve the position of chief marketing officer in a manufacturing company with at least $250 million in annual revenue

- To be running your own equity portfolio at one of the ten largest fund-management firms by age 35

- To own your own ad agency, with at least $15 million in annual billings in 15 years

- To be promoted to corporate treasurer at your current employer by the end of next year

Note that all of these goals are fairly specific. Specific goals focus your mind and energies. Also, for each of these goals you would need interim objectives. Those objectives help you break things down into manageable stages, get you thinking about preparation and provide markers to measure your progress or to signal the need for a change of direction.

Tips for Setting Goals:

- Put them in writing. Studies have shown that people who have their goals in writing achieve them far more often than people who don't.

- Make your goals ambitious but attainable. If you fall short of high aims, you will still have accomplished something worthwhile. Also, ambitious goals will inspire you.

- Share your goals with your spouse and, if appropriate, your family and close friends. Doing so will engender greater support while giving others an opportunity to state their opinions or needs.

Preparation: Conduct Research and Development

Planning is mentally bringing the future into the present so you can visualize the results you want and decide how to create them. To prepare a career plan, first visualize your career goals and then research and develop ways and means of reaching them.

You might think of this as R&D for your career. Too many people run their careers like companies that focus only on daily operations and fail to invest in R&D. Those companies (and people) often short-change their futures. Research—the R in R&D—means researching the resources needed to reach your goals. For instance, you may need certain credentials or skills, such as an MBA or fluency in Mandarin, or partners or financing for a business. Identify the resources you'll need well in advance. Development—the D in R&D—means developing the resources you've identified. Will your employer pay for your MBA and otherwise support your efforts to obtain one? What's the best way to learn Mandarin, and how can you get started? Who might be likely sources of financing for your business?

Also, have plans B and C. Things change. Stuff happens. Even entire industries come and go. Your plan must be flexible and allow for the unexpected.

Tips for Preparing Your Plan:

- Take an open and thorough approach to ways and means of achieving your goals. The first path you identify may not be the best path.

- Use the Internet, libraries, magazines and experts as sources. Approach experts *after* doing some research; they are understandably annoyed when people ask questions answered in any basic book on their subject.

- Don't overspecialize, but be specific. By that we mean, don't choose too narrow a path because if you find it blocked, you may not find a way around the barrier. For instance, if you want a position in financial services in London, don't reflexively pass up Hong Kong or Frankfurt, which could lead to a position in London.

- Discuss your plan with a knowledgeable friend or buy a few hours of a career counselor's time. You will get some good feedback and new ideas.

Action: Just Do It

We've covered some of the things you must do to attain a senior-level position: embody excellence, choose employers wisely, develop a network and become known in your industry. These things don't just happen; you make them happen through your actions.

Most people fail to achieve their long-term goals not because they are unable to set them or don't want to fulfill them badly enough, but simply because they fail to act effectively. They do not connect their daily actions to their long-term goals. They let the urgent crowd out the important. Urgent matters will always demand immediate attention, so you must consciously focus on the long-term. Working on long-term goals calls for time management, also known as setting priorities. Do you watch television? Spend time in unproductive meetings? How do you use the time you spend commuting? Most of us feel we are going flat out much of the time. However, acting on your career goals means more than doing a good day's work. It means optimizing your effort to make future days better.

Tips for Taking Action:

- Get help in pursuing your career goals. Cultivate mentors as well as colleagues and contacts (and mentor others). Everyone who has achieved outstanding success has had help.

- If you study successful executives, you'll find that very few of them react to every little thing. They distinguish between the big picture and the smudge in the corner, and allocate their time accordingly. Apply the 80/20 rule: Spend 80 percent of your time on the 20 percent of things that are truly important.

- Take at least one or two actions every week to move toward your longer term goals. Schedule the activities—skill development, networking, writing articles and so on—that will move you ahead.

Assessment/Adjustment: Keep on Track

Too many plans in business are placed in the lower left-hand drawer, never to be seen again. Don't consign your career plan to that fate. Periodically consult your plan and monitor your progress. If you lack interest in your plan, ask yourself why. Were your goals ambitious enough? Or were they too ambitious? Was it really *your* plan? Or was it what you thought should be your plan?

When you review your plan and your progress, look for what you're doing right, what you're doing wrong and what you're not doing. Are you where the action is in your organization? If not, how can you get there? Are you seeing regular promotions? Are you developing contacts and mentors? Do you feel progress or stasis? And so on.

If your progress is slow or you feel you're losing ground (and time), examine your goals, preparation and actions. Overhaul the plan if necessary. Address the areas that need correction. But also realize that everyone experiences a setback, failure or bad year now and then. The only security is in a rut. In fact, even a rut is no longer a safe place to be.

Tips for Assessing Progress:

- Don't abandon a treasured goal because of difficulties. In most endeavors, persistence will eventually win the day, even over talent and intelligence.

- If you hit a wall or feel real frustration, talk it over with someone you trust and respect. Often the simple act of talking it out will help you see a way forward.

- When you find yourself behind your timetable, step back and look at the progress you have made. Are you moving toward your goals? What does the delay mean in the context of your entire career? Keep things in perspective, and if you are achieving your goals, don't worry too much about being late.

- Be aware of the trade-offs you may be making in other areas of your life. If you have a family, ask yourself: How's your marriage? When you go home, do your children recognize you? Remember the old *New Yorker* cartoon: At a cocktail party, one executive says to another, "I've learned an awful lot in my 40 years with Amalgamated. Unfortunately, it's all about aluminum."

PATHS TO THE TOP

In most organizations, some paths are more likely than others to lead to a senior management position. The likeliest route might include a particular function such as finance or marketing, or a particular skill such as knowing the numbers or being a rainmaker, or even an area of the company such as the Paris office or the South American operation. When you interview with an organization, ask about the paths that the senior executives took to their positions. Some company cultures include the belief that an executive needs certain very specific experience. Lack of that experience may hinder your progress toward a desired position.

It may be possible to compensate for that lack. In a sales-driven culture, for example, no matter which function you oversee, be sure to establish and maintain contact with sales managers and customers, perhaps through marketing, product development or special projects. If a stint in Paris or South America is considered essential, try to arrange for a tour of duty there, or at least visit and get to know people in those organizational outposts.

The path to the top is now often nonlinear. Few executives go from marketing manager to marketing director to marketing vice president, senior vice president and executive vice president in the same company. A typical career will include moves among a few companies. Note, however, that most executives at substantial, well-established organizations have typically spent enough time in one company to build the knowledge, relationships and power needed to make a major contribution.

THE TRUE EXECUTIVE

In the past two or three decades, the world of work has been transformed along with the world itself. Yet one thing hasn't changed: Organizations large and small, in the public and private sectors, need skilled senior executives. This becomes most obvious when a company fails. In that unfortunate event, senior management has misjudged the market, neglected the customer, adopted the wrong technology, ignored unpleasant facts, tolerated unethical practices or violated basic management principles.

True executives do the opposite. They face reality, consider the good of the company and its stakeholders and decide and act on the basis of facts and management principles. Senior management is one of the toughest jobs in business, far more difficult than it appears to people outside organizational life, and even to some inside. It demands as much energy and maturity as it does knowledge and skills.

Retained search consultants help companies locate true executives. They also help those executives toward positions where they can make their greatest contribution and earn their greatest rewards. We trust that this guide has clarified the potential role of retained executive search in your organization and career. If you would like more information about executive search, please visit the Association of Executive Search Consultants' websites at www.aesc.org and www.bluesteps.com. There you will find a wealth of knowledge on the subject as well as contact and other information on the AESC and its members.

ACTION POINTS

- Manage your career with the understanding that no one will manage it for you. Few companies provide employment or financial security as they once did.

- Begin your career-management initiative with an honest, written self-inventory. The more explicitly you identify your motivations, the more intelligently you will be able to make career choices.

- In executing your career plan, define your goals, make the necessary preparations, take action and periodically assess your progress and make adjustments as needed.

- Think of preparation as R&D for your career. You must research and develop the skills, experience and other resources that you will require to reach your career goals.

- Be aware of the paths to the top in your organization and try to take, or at least touch, one of those paths during your career there. Also, accept the reality of organizational politics and take a positive approach based on facts and data, while building relationships and alliances.

- Learn more about managing your career and the role that executive search can play in your efforts—and in your organization—by visiting www.aesc.org and www.bluesteps.com.

The Candidate's Bill of Rights

Copyright © 2002 by the Association of Executive Search Consultants

WHAT TO EXPECT FROM A PROFESSIONAL EXECUTIVE SEARCH FIRM

It often happens when you least expect it. Out of the blue you receive a call from an executive search firm, wanting to know if you might have an interest in a position they are trying to fill for a client.

The opportunity seems promising, but you do not know what to expect. What does the process entail? How long will it take? What will the search firm expect from you? Most important, what are your rights and obligations during the process? As a potential search candidate, you are entitled to ask these questions and to have them answered.

In retained executive search, consultants endeavor to provide qualified candidates for clients who wish to fill senior-level positions. Although contractual obligations exist only between the search firm and client, search consultants also build professional and ethical relationships with candidates, whom they may remain in contact with over a period of years.

Members of the Association of Executive Search Consultants (AESC), the worldwide professional organization for retained executive search firms, subscribe to a code of ethics that states that these relationships should be characterized by honesty, objectivity, accuracy and respect for confidentiality. Strict adherence to this code is a requirement for all AESC members, who must also abide by all data privacy laws applicable within their country.

Furthermore, AESC members believe that the most successful executive searches involve a three-way partnership, whereby the candidate, the search firm and the client fully understand their rights, duties and obligations to each other during the search process. As such, we believe that all search candidates have the following rights.

THE CANDIDATE'S BILL OF RIGHTS

I. Confidentiality

When you become an executive search candidate, you put yourself at a certain amount of risk with your current employer. For that reason, you are entitled to the highest levels of confidentiality from the search firm and the client organization. To safeguard your confidentiality, the search consultant should:

- Following a meeting to discuss your candidacy, obtain your authorization before submitting your name and a report on you to the client organization.

- Upon your request, contact you directly rather than through your assistant or anyone else in your current company.

- Not contact references provided by you without your permission.

- Not discuss your potential candidacy with anyone outside the search firm, and ensure

that all employees of the firm abide by the
same rules.

- Caution the client to also safeguard your confidentiality.

It is important to remember that you do not become
a search candidate until the consultant has conducted an
initial evaluation of your suitability for the position *and*
you have expressed an interest in it. If either of these two
criteria are missing, you cannot be considered a candidate for the position. However, even if the position about
which you are being contacted is not right for you at the
present time, you may still benefit from conversations
with search consultants by being kept up to date with
the market for your skills and experience. Candidates not
selected on one search may be selected on another.

II. Full Disclosure

In order to make the right decision, you need to know as
much as possible about the search firm you are talking to,
the position and the client organization. This ultimately
requires full and open disclosure regarding:

- The nature and requirements of the position

- The compensation package

- Whether relocation is required

- Pertinent information regarding the client organization

Be aware, however, that during your first conversation, when you are still being evaluated as a potential candidate for the position, the search consultant is under no obligation to divulge confidential information about the position or the client. Only after you have been identified as a legitimate candidate should you expect the consultant to disclose more than the most basic information. Even then, there are times when certain information about the client must remain confidential until the final stages of the search process.

The search consultant should also make clear whether he or she has been *retained* by the client to manage the appointment in question. Retained executive search consultants work under an exclusive contract with the client organization; and thus have not only confidential access to the client on that assignment but have their full and committed attention. If the consultant fails to notify you of this important fact, do not hesitate to ask.

III. Timely Communication

The completion of an executive search assignment can often take several months, with many steps between initial contact and the ultimate hiring of the successful candidate. Once you become an active candidate, the search firm should communicate with you in a timely manner at each and every step of the process. This means proactively updating you on the progress of the search as well as responding in a timely manner to any inquiries initiated by you.

IV. Feedback

Based on his or her understanding of the position and the client's needs, the search consultant should give you an honest appraisal of where you seem to fit the opportunity and where you do not seem to fit. If at any point in the process the client decides not to proceed with your candidacy, the consultant should provide as complete an explanation of the client's decision as possible.

V. Professional Treatment

Search consultants are expected to comply with all the employment laws that apply to the normal hiring process. In addition, they should also demonstrate a high level of professionalism with each and every candidate. Professional treatment means that the search consultant:

- Has a clear understanding of the position and the client's expectations for it

- Conducts an organized, well-thought-out interview

- Shows up on time and well-prepared for all appointments

- Demonstrates in-depth knowledge of the market and the client

- Answers all your questions in an honest and forthright manner

VI. Adequate Process Details

As a search candidate, you are entitled to know what to expect as the process unfolds. For example, what is the anticipated time frame for the first round of interviews? If you make the first cut, what happens next? Most search consultants will readily volunteer this kind of information. If they do not, make a point to ask. In particular, be prepared at any stage in the proceedings to ask:

- How long will this take?

- Who do I have to meet with before a decision is made?

- What time frame is the client working on?

- What is the next step?

VII. Respect for Your Time and Position

The search consultant understands that, as a senior level executive, your current position demands your full time and attention. When scheduling appointments and interviews, the search consultant and the client should demonstrate the utmost respect for your time, your position and your responsibilities to your employer.

VIII. Consistency Between the Search Firm and Their Client

The search consultant and the client should always do their best to be on the same wavelength in terms of the information they present to you. Keep in mind, however, that while the search consultant represents the client organization, they do not have complete control over the client's communication with you during the process. If changes occur that contradict the information given to you by the consultant, you should ask for clarification.

IX. No Pressure

The best executive search placements happen when the candidate has the time to make a measured, well-thought-out decision. For this reason, the search consultant should never try to hurry your decision or put undue pressure on you to accept an offer. However, the consultant should keep you informed of any deadlines imposed by the client and the implications for not making a decision prior to those deadlines.

X. A Trusting Relationship

If the search consultant conducts him or herself in a manner befitting these guiding principles, you should naturally develop an open and trusting relationship. Conversely, if for any reason you do not feel you can trust the search consultant or the client, you would be well served to withdraw from the process. Keep in mind that the best search consultants strive for more than just filling the position for their client; they want to help you make the best decision for you, your family and your career.

CONCLUDING THE SEARCH

If the client decides to hire you to fill the position, you have arrived at one of the most important stages of the search process: negotiation of your employment agreement. This can involve highly sensitive issues in which the search consultant can play a crucial role of intermediary to ensure open and effective communication between client and candidate. Use this "honest broker" channel of communication to candidly express any concerns or special requirements that you may have on terms and conditions.

When the search process is completed and you have signed on the dotted line, some search consultants will stay in touch with you for three to six months to make sure that your transition into the new position is a success. Feel free to contact your consultant with major concerns that arise. He or she may well be able to help sort out problems, and diplomatic intervention by the search consultant will normally not be resented by the client. However, search consultants are not professional coaches, and thus their role here may be limited.

If your candidacy does not result in a hire, most consultants will want to keep you in their pool of candidates for future assignments. They may contact you from time to time to maintain the relationship and keep you appraised of any upcoming assignments. They may also use you as a resource to help identify candidates for assignments that are not a good fit for you. If you developed a good relationship with the search consultant, you may want to take your own steps to maintain the relationship as well.

Regardless of the outcome of the search, the consultant may not use your name or the results of the search as testimonials without your permission.

PUTTING YOUR BEST FOOT FORWARD

The executive search process is not a one-way street. Although you have a right to expect courteous, professional treatment from the search consultant and the client, there are a number of things you can do to facilitate the process and advance your standing.

- **Be honest.** Under no circumstances should you inflate your resume, misrepresent your work history or "hold some cards back." Also, be genuine about your interest (or lack of) in the position. Complete and accurate disclosure by the candidate is an essential element in the search process.

- **Be flexible.** Make every effort to fit appointments and interviews within your schedule.

- **Educate yourself.** Conduct your own due diligence on the search firm and the client organization, and understand the unique value of retained executive search consulting.

- **Have realistic expectations.** Understand that the process takes time and that you will be one of several qualified candidates.

- **Negotiate in good faith.** Do not lead search consultants to believe you are negotiating only with them if you are considering offers from more than one organization.

Above all, do not think you have a "done deal" just because you develop a close relationship with the search consultant. Remember that the consultant's job is to present several qualified candidates to the client, and it is the client who makes the ultimate decision.

MAKING THE CONNECTION

How do you get on the "radar screen" of leading search firms around the world? One of the best ways is to register with BlueSteps, a service of the Association of Executive Search Consultants. Doing so will raise your visibility with the most appropriate search firms in an efficient, economical and confidential manner. It will also ensure that any search firms who contact you from the BlueSteps global database subscribe to the highest ethics and standards as put forth by the AESC.

The more you know about the executive search process, the better you can position yourself should you become an executive search candidate. In the meantime, remember that the most successful executive searches involve those where you, the search consultant and the client know your rights and obligations within the search process and adhere to the highest standards of professional and ethical conduct.

This document is also available on the AESC websites: www.aesc.org and www.bluesteps.com.